Scream Machines

ALL ABOUT ROLLER COASTERS

By Susan Schott Karr

Photographs by Paul L. Ruben

CELEBRATION PRESS

Pearson Learning Group

CONTENTS

THE THRILL OF THE RIDE

From a distance, the steel roller coaster looks like a tangle of color and curves cutting into the vivid blue sky. This hypercoaster—a coaster that is higher than 200 feet—is famous worldwide for its loops and corkscrews. It's known as one of the best "scream machines" at this amusement park.

You rush to the loading station and find a seat in the first car. It's hard to contain your excitement. An endless double line of steep, green tracks stretches before you. As the cars lurch out of the station, your hands grip the safety bar tightly. The coaster seems to take forever to climb up the first hill. Next to you, your friend says, "You know, I'm not sure I want to do this after all."

The Incredible Hulk Coaster® at Universal's Islands of Adventure℠ in Orlando, Florida

You just grin. You know it's too late to turn back now, and besides, you *want* to be frightened. After all, that's part of the excitement and the fun. You push your head back against the headrest and scream as loudly as you can.

Everybody else seems to be screaming, too. Then suddenly, after you've rounded the peak of the first hill, you see the track plunging down before you, as if it's perpendicular to the ground below.

As you race downhill at 70 miles per hour, you wonder if your heart might jump into your throat. At the bottom of the hill, you feel oddly heavy, as if you weigh several times your normal weight. You don't have long to think about this strange sensation, because now you're climbing uphill again.

At the top of the next hill, you feel completely weightless, as if your body would float out of the car if you weren't strapped in by your seat belt and lap restraint. You look down at the ground, yet this is no time for sightseeing. The coaster continues to whip around the track, giving you more of a thrill than you could have imagined.

Suddenly, without warning, the coaster rounds a sharply banked turn. Your body presses into the side of the car as if you might melt right through it.

You hear your friend yell, "I'm shutting my eyes! This is horrible!" You're laughing too hard to take her seriously.

When the coaster enters its first loop, the train flies up toward the clouds. It's a good thing you're strapped in tightly and the coaster's wheels are locked to the track. Before you can catch your breath again, you've lost any sense of where the ground is. You can't even tell if you're right-side up or upside down.

It seems as if your ride began just milliseconds ago, yet now the coaster returns to the station. It's time to climb out of the car and steady your feet on the ground. This was the best ride you've ever taken, and already you're thinking about getting back in line to do it again.

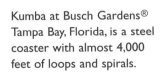

Kumba at Busch Gardens® Tampa Bay, Florida, is a steel coaster with almost 4,000 feet of loops and spirals.

For over 500 years, people have sought the thrill of a ride on a roller coaster. The roller coaster is a machine that uses **gravity** and **momentum** to perform its drops and loops. Its design has changed over the years as new materials and technology have improved and as safety features have been added. Still, people come back to these scream machines for the same reasons: the thrill of racing down from great heights, the feeling of weightlessness at the top of a hill, and the sense of being out of control.

When you're riding a roller coaster, you may not think about anything except the excitement of the ride and the butterflies in your stomach. In fact, though, a lot of science has gone into creating your fun.

When you're plunging down a hill, speed and **acceleration** add to the rush your body is feeling. When you turn upside down on a loop, gravity is pulling your body down. At the same time, **centripetal force**, the force that keeps an object moving toward the inside of a circle, is making sure you won't fall out of your car! Designers consider all these forces when they build coasters. In fact, designers have been improving coasters since the early 1500s. That's when roller coasters got their start, on icy hills in Russia.

ROLLER COASTERS THEN AND NOW

The history of the roller coaster begins in the 1500s in Saint Petersburg, Russia. During the long, cold winters, Russians packed snow onto wooden ramps. They watered down the ramps, turning the surface into ice. Then the fun began.

People climbed 70 feet (five stories) up a wooden ladder or a set of steps to sleds. These were made of wood or ice and were padded with straw seats. The sleds hurtled down the tracks at 50 miles per hour (mph), earning the nickname "Flying Mountains." Ice sliding remained popular for over 200 years.

Catherine the Great was empress of Russia in the late 1700s. She was certain that ice sliding could be made into warm-weather fun for the many nobles who visited at her summer palace.

Russian citizens go ice sliding in Saint Petersburg, Russia, in 1610. (Paul L. Ruben archives)

Coaster History

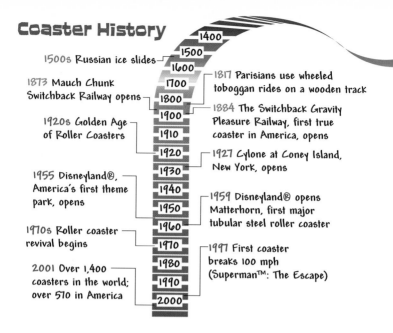

1400
1500
1600
1700
1800
1900
1910
1920
1930
1940
1950
1960
1970
1980
1990
2000

1500s Russian ice slides

1873 Mauch Chunk Switchback Railway opens

1920s Golden Age of Roller Coasters

1955 Disneyland®, America's first theme park, opens

1970s Roller coaster revival begins

2001 Over 1,400 coasters in the world; over 510 in America

1817 Parisians use wheeled toboggan rides on a wooden track

1884 The Switchback Gravity Pleasure Railway, first true coaster in America, opens

1927 Cylone at Coney Island, New York, opens

1959 Disneyland® opens Matterhorn, first major tubular steel roller coaster

1997 First coaster breaks 100 mph (Superman™: The Escape)

First, Catherine the Great had her workers build outdoor wooden tracks. Then they put small wheels on the bottom of sleds. This let the sleds roll down dry tracks without having to depend on the cold and ice. Her guests climbed three stories to the top of a terrace. Over and over again, they rolled down the steep tracks on their sleds.

In the early nineteenth century, a French traveler went to Russia. He brought the idea of roller coasters back to his country. Like Catherine the Great, the French put tiny wheels on the vehicles. They called these sleds "Russian Mountains."

By 1873, in the mountains of Pennsylvania, Americans had tried out their own roller coaster.

This came to be known as the Mauch Chunk Switchback Railway (or Railroad). It was first built for coal miners. They had used mules to pull an empty train to the top of a mountain. At the peak, they loaded the train cars with coal. Then the train hauled the coal downhill. The train traveled 9 miles to the landing in the town of Mauch Chunk, now called Jim Thorpe.

When the cars were emptied of coal, the miners found that they could use the cars for a fun-filled ride. Riders were willing to pay 50 cents a ride to roll downhill. They often sat sideways in the cars as they wheeled along the trail and came to a halt. The mules rode too!

In the late 1800s, riders rode the Mauch Chunk Switchback Railway down a mountain in Pennsylvania.

In 1884, at Coney Island in New York, La Marcus A. Thompson built the first American roller coaster that was just for entertainment. He called it Switchback Railway and charged 5 cents a ride. Although its top speed was 6 mph, the 10-car, 600-foot coaster was so popular that it paid for itself in 3 weeks.

By the 1920s, roller coasting was all the rage. People were eager for something new in the era of the Roaring Twenties. The decade was also known as the Golden Age of Roller Coasters.

It was during this golden age, in 1927, that the Cyclone was built at Coney Island. With its steep first drop and a rattling ride, the Cyclone became the most famous roller coaster in the world.

By 1929, the United States was home to about 1,500 to 2,000 coasters, but this soon changed. The stock market crashed, the Great Depression took hold, and then World War II began. Thousands of people lost their jobs and no longer had as much money for recreation. Roller coasting entered its darkest age. It was hard to find materials, and the building of roller coasters nearly came to a halt. Hundreds of coasters were torn down.

During the 1930s and 1940s, many amusement parks in America were shut down. Roller coasting had lost the grand appeal it had held for so long.

The wooden Cyclone at Astroland Amusement Park, Coney Island, New York, opened in 1927.

Then, in the 1950s, roller coasting came to life again as new amusement parks began to appear around the country. As the number of parks grew, so did the number of roller coasters. Once again, Americans had the chance to enjoy the thrill of riding their favorite coasters. They started to call the roller coaster the scream machine.

Although by 1960 there were only 200 coasters in the United States, new designers and builders were at work. They went on to build bigger, better, and more creative roller coasters.

Walt Disney had opened Disneyland® park in California in 1955. Disneyland introduced the first modern steel roller coaster, the Matterhorn Bobsleds, in 1959. By using steel as a building material, designers could imagine and build ever more fantastic scream machines.

The use of steel led to the creation of some trend-setting coasters. In 1975, the Corkscrew at Knott's® Berry Farm in Buena Park, California, opened as the first modern looping coaster. By 1984, parks had opened successful **suspended roller coasters**—coasters with enclosed cars that hang beneath the track—and stand-up coasters. With safety restraints over their shoulders and the promise of an intense ride, riders of stand-up coasters stand in rows in the car as the coaster whips around the track.

Superman™: The Escape was the first coaster to hit 100 mph. It premiered in 1997 at Six Flags® Magic Mountain in Valencia, California.

Today, there are over 1,400 coasters in the world, and over 570 of them are in the United States. Without a doubt, roller coasters have entered another golden age.

Superman™: The Escape at Six Flags® Magic Mountain, Valencia, California, became the first coaster to go 100 miles per hour.

HOW DO COASTERS WORK?

What makes a roller coaster work? As the roller coaster leaves the station, its motion and the forces that drive it differ from those that power a train. While a train is propelled along the tracks by an engine, most roller coasters depend on gravity for power. From the start, a roller coaster needs to build up enough energy for its entire ride.

At first, a motor powers a chain to move the coaster up the first hill, or lift hill, as it's called. Then, in the longest drop the coaster will take during its ride, gravity pulls the cars toward the Earth. For the rest of the ride, the roller coaster coasts along its track. This "coasting" gives the roller coaster its name.

As the roller coaster moves up the lift hill, it is storing energy for the way down. When the coaster moves forward on its own, it uses the energy of its movement to keep itself going.

As the roller coaster moves along the track, the force of friction begins to slow it down and use up the coaster's energy. Friction is caused by the whipping of the wind on the cars and riders and by the contact of the wheels with the track. The fact that a roller coaster is able to roll instead of

one G
(rider feels normal)

zero Gs
(rider feels weightless)

Lift Hill

two Gs
(rider feels twice as
heavy as normal)

slide reduces some—but not all—of the friction.

Because friction slows down the coaster, each
new hill after the lift hill must be lower than the one
before. If the train is going to make it all the way
back to the station, it must have enough energy to
complete the trip.

When the roller coaster rounds a turn in the
track, riders feel centripetal force. They may feel
pushed to the inside or the outside of the car.
Designers know just how to build up the track to
counteract this centripetal force.

As the coaster lurches over the top of a hill and
plunges down to its lowest points, another type of
force is at work. Gravity forces, or **G-forces**, are
measured in "Gs." One G-force is equal to the force

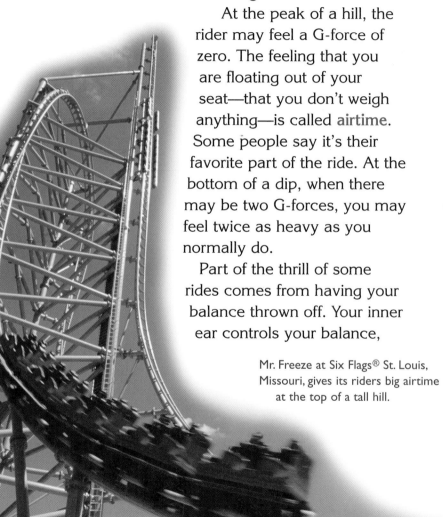

of gravity when a rider is at rest, but this changes at points along the ride. G-forces have different effects on how the rider's body feels, depending on where the coaster is along the ride.

At the peak of a hill, the rider may feel a G-force of zero. The feeling that you are floating out of your seat—that you don't weigh anything—is called airtime. Some people say it's their favorite part of the ride. At the bottom of a dip, when there may be two G-forces, you may feel twice as heavy as you normally do.

Part of the thrill of some rides comes from having your balance thrown off. Your inner ear controls your balance,

Mr. Freeze at Six Flags® St. Louis, Missouri, gives its riders big airtime at the top of a tall hill.

and it lets you know which way is right-side up. Sometimes during a roller coaster ride, your inner ear may not seem to work. As the coaster whips around a loop, you can't be sure where the ground is or if you're right-side up or upside down.

Designers use their knowledge of how coasters work as well as their creativity to come up with new ideas. They like to find ways to make the scream machines as unpredictable and as hair-raising as possible. They put a lot of thought into the "fun business."

DESIGNING A SCREAM MACHINE

It's not easy to build a roller coaster, make sure it works, and provide enough fear and fun to the ride—while keeping it safe for its riders.

Designers start by doing research. Part of the job is to decide what type of rides a park wants and what kind of materials to use in each coaster.

The designers work with the people who build the roller coaster. Roller coasters are made of either wood or steel. Both design and building depend on whether the train will be a "woodie" or a "steelie." Each type has its own features and its own "feel" during the ride.

Until the 1950s, coasters rode on wooden tracks that were much like railroad tracks. Then, in 1959, when tubular steel tracks were built, steel coasters came into being. Although a steel coaster runs on a steel track, the support

Millennium Force™ at Cedar Point, Ohio, has a 310-foot-high lift hill!

structure, just as with a wooden coaster, can be either steel or wood.

Woodies usually rattle and bump along. Their tracks give them a lot of room to move around, and they treat their riders to a noisy clatter and a swaying motion.

Steelies, on the other hand, give a smooth, tight ride. The wheels ride close to the tracks. With steelies, designers could add safe loops, with places where riders turn upside down. Steelies also gave designers the chance to build rides where people stand up or take a free fall. During free fall, the coaster plunges downward, and riders feel only the force of gravity.

Lightning Racer™ at HERSHEYPARK™ in Pennsylvania is a wooden coaster with a double track.

Some features are common to all coasters. For instance, they usually have three sets of wheels. This helps to manage the movement of the cars along the track. The under-friction wheels run under the track and hold the cars to the track. The guide wheels run on the sides of the track and help guide the cars. The road wheels run on top of the track and carry the cars.

Just like any train, a roller coaster must have a set of brakes. However, the brakes on a roller coaster differ from those of a train. They are built into the track, not into the coaster.

Not all coasters use a lift hill to get started. One new type of launcher uses **compressed air**. Air that has been under high pressure is released, pushing off the coaster. Another new launcher uses a magnetic motor to launch the coasters like a slingshot. It's called **linear induction motor (LIM)**. At Six Flags® St. Louis and Six Flags® Over Texas, the Mr. Freeze coasters use LIM. There is a magnetic "wave" along the track, and the cars are pushed ahead of the wave with magnets attached to the bottom of the cars.

Designers use certain "tricks" to create the illusion of danger and the feeling of fear. For starters, they make the first climb on the lift hill slow. Because it seems to take forever to get to the

American Roller Coaster Records

WOODEN ROLLER COASTERS	STEEL ROLLER COASTERS
LONGEST: **THE BEAST®** Paramount's Kings Island Kings Island, OH Length: 7,400 feet	**LONGEST:** **MILLENNIUM FORCE™** Cedar Point Sandusky, OH Length: 6,595 feet
TALLEST: **SON OF BEAST™** Paramount's Kings Island Kings Island, OH Height: 218 feet	**TALLEST:** **SUPERMAN™: THE ESCAPE** Six Flags® Magic Mountain Valencia, CA Height: 415 feet
FASTEST: **SON OF BEAST™** Paramount's Kings Island Kings Island, OH Speed: 78 mph	**FASTEST:** **SUPERMAN™: THE ESCAPE** Six Flags® Magic Mountain Valencia, CA Speed: 100 mph
GREATEST DROP: **SON OF BEAST™** Paramount's Kings Island Kings Island, OH Drop: 214 feet	**GREATEST DROP:** **SUPERMAN™: THE ESCAPE** Six Flags® Magic Mountain Valencia, CA Drop: 328 feet, 1 inch

Other Records

OLDEST COASTER **STILL RUNNING:** **LEAP-THE-DIPS** Lakemont Park Altoona, PA Built 1902
MOST FAMOUS: **CYCLONE** Astroland Amusement Park Coney Island, Brooklyn, NY Opened: 1927 Speed: 60 mph
PARKS WITH THE MOST **ROLLER COASTERS:** **SIX FLAGS®** **MAGIC MOUNTAIN** Valencia, CA **CEDAR POINT** Sandusky, OH Number: 15 each

peak, you may think you're going up higher than you really are. You have more time to squirm!

During a ride, a coaster may go slowly at some points, so the designer adds curves and builds up the turns to make you think you're going faster. To make turns seem sharper than they really are, the designer may put trees, poles, or a tunnel close to the track.

Part of the challenge of building roller coasters is to create new designs, such as those for looping, suspended, and inverted coasters. When a part of the track causes the cars to travel upside

Montu at Busch Gardens® Tampa Bay, Florida, lets its riders know the real meaning of *inversion*.

down, it's called an **inversion**. Loops are one kind of inversion. A corkscrew is an inversion that has a twist in it and circles upon itself.

The enclosed cars of suspended coasters swing from side to side as the coaster moves and takes the curves. Like suspended coasters, inverted coasters also hang from a track, but the cars are open. The riders' legs hang down.

Some of the advances in design are due to the use of computer technology. With computers, designers can build coasters that are higher, faster, and filled with more surprises than ever before. Computers also help designers to balance the sense of danger with a promise of safety.

ARE ROLLER COASTERS SAFE?

The earliest roller coasting was fun, but it was also very dangerous. In Russia, the hills were so steep, a guide sometimes rode along to help the rider steer the coaster.

In Paris in the early 1800s, when the Russian Mountains were built, little care was given to safety. Because the tracks were so steep and the coasters went so fast, there were many accidents. Coasters were likely to shoot off the track without any warning.

This risk did not stop people from riding these freewheeling coasters. On the contrary, even more people came to watch and to ride. The thought of danger made the sport all the more exciting.

The appeal of danger was also popular during the golden age of roller coasting, the 1920s. In 1927, a designer named Harry Guy Traver decided to take coasting to the extreme.

Traver built three coasters that he called the Giant Cyclone Safety Coasters. All three were about 100 feet tall. Each had turns that were so steep, the track was almost perpendicular to the ground.

On Traver's wooden Cyclone coasters, there was no way to be sure that the riders would not fall out or get hurt. It was not unusual for riders to break their bones or faint during the ride. One park kept a nurse on hand just to care for people who fainted or got hurt. The publicity made fear fans eager to try out the coaster.

John A. Miller, an American coaster designer and builder, was one of the first people to make roller coasters safe. He invented a number of safety devices, including under-friction wheels, locking bars, and anti-rollback devices.

Miller patented the under-friction wheels in 1912. They kept the car on the track. Locking bars held the riders in the car so they would not go flying into the air. Anti-rollback devices kept the cars from slipping backward on the track. Miller's inventions are still used in today's coasters.

Kumba at Busch Gardens® Tampa Bay, Florida, uses under-friction wheels, along with two other sets of wheels.

Miller designed roller coasters and coaster safety devices before there were computers. Modern technology and better building materials have led to safer rides. Even so, some dangers may still exist in today's roller coasters.

With new kinds of coasters now in the parks, riders can feel up to 5 or 6 Gs. But is this safe? Some people are worried that high G-forces can cause riders' brains to shake around in their skulls. Some riders have said that riding extreme coasters damaged their brains.

A member of Congress, Representative Edward Markey of Massachusetts, is looking into the matter. He wants to pass a National Amusement Park Ride Safety Act. The law would allow the Consumer Product Safety Commission (CPSC) to inspect and watch over roller coaster rides. It would also limit the number of G-forces on coasters.

Today, each state has to make its own safety laws. In New Jersey, lawmakers have set limits on how long a ride can hurl its riders left and right or pull a person up or down. They hope that other states will also agree on G-force limits.

What do amusement park officials say about coaster safety? They point to the millions of riders who ride their coasters without having an accident. Many also say that if riders get hurt, it is because they were not healthy enough to go on the rides or did not follow the rules for safety.

Parks do post their rules. Still, people don't always follow them. Riders are often warned to secure their loose objects, but people have lost everything from keys to false teeth while riding roller coasters. How many times have you seen people riding a roller coaster and holding their hands up in the air? They are ignoring the most basic safety rule.

Smart riders know that they can stay safe and have a great time. Here are some tips from safety experts for staying safe on roller coasters.

- Follow all posted rules for age and height.
- Listen to instructions from ride operators.
- Keep your arms, legs, hands, and long hair inside your car.
- Always use your seat belt, lap bar, and shoulder harness.
- Hold on to the handrails.
- Stay in the car until it comes to a full stop.
- Stop boarding rides *before* you get too tired.

IN SEARCH OF THE "BEST" RIDES

The best rides are not always the biggest, the longest, or the fastest. Roller coaster fans may want to try the most extreme rides or the newest rides when they visit an amusement park. However, those rides aren't necessarily the ones that riders will visit over and over again. What keeps fans coming back to the same coasters?

Although steelies are newer and have more features, many roller coaster fans still love good old woodies. They like the way the cars rattle and rock along the track. Steelies, on the other hand, give riders a smoother—and sometimes quieter—ride. Let's take a look at three woodies and three steelies that riders in one poll thought were "the best."

As the longest wooden coaster in the world at 7,400 feet, The Beast® gives its riders a ride that lasts nearly five minutes. This coaster at Paramount's Kings Island in Kings Island, Ohio, opened in 1979 and has held its record for over 20 years. It has not one, but two, lifts to keep it going.

There's something else that makes this coaster special. It was built away from the main park in 35 acres of woods. Because it's in the woods, riders of The Beast don't always know what's

The Beast® at Paramount's Kings Island in Kings Island, Ohio, is the world's longest wooden coaster.

around the next turn. They may be surprised by a dark underground tunnel or the stomach-turning finale. After coming out of the last tunnel, riders are taken around a large circle of track in a helix. On this ride, the excitement never lets up.

Fans of The Beast are also often fans of its "son." Located in the same amusement park, Son of Beast™ is the only looping wooden coaster in the world.

The track twists and turns, plunges and soars. Launched in 2000, it has a speed that peaks at over 78 mph. Son of Beast has two amazing drops and, at one point, a G-force of 4.5. The ride lasts a little over two minutes, but what it lacks in time, it makes up for in airtime and that upside-down feeling. This ride is proof that old-fashioned woodies are still thrilling.

The Thunderbolt at Kennywood Park in Pennsylvania is known for its 90-foot final drop.

In 1924, John Miller built a coaster called the Pippin. Then, in 1968, Andy Vettel changed the design and opened it as the Thunderbolt. When the Thunderbolt leaves the station, instead of going up a lift hill, this coaster drops its riders into a ravine. But another surprise is yet to come. One of the longest drops on the Thunderbolt is the last one!

The Thunderbolt is known as a classic coaster. The cars are wide open, and it contains no seat dividers or head restraints. People who enjoy the feel of an old-fashioned woodie say this is one of the best rides ever.

The Incredible Hulk Coaster® is a looping steel

coaster that is named after the comic book character. Located in Orlando, Florida, this coaster starts in an enclosed lift hill. In just two seconds after leaving the loading station, the lift launches the train from zero to 40 mph. Next, without any warning, it propels its riders with enough momentum to ensure that the train will get through the corkscrew at the top of the ride.

All together, this scream machine has seven inversions. These include two vertical loops, two barrel rolls, one zero-gravity roll, and one cobra roll. On the cobra roll, the track makes a sharp turn that looks like the head of a cobra.

Millennium Force™ became a quick hit when it opened in 2000. This one-of-a-kind hypercoaster was built at Cedar Point, Ohio. No sooner do riders get to the top of the 310-foot lift hill then they drop 300 feet at an 80-degree angle. This coaster swoops riders through tunnels, around tight turns, and down sharp drops.

Millennium Force has three trains that all run on the track at the same time. The trains lean so far over, riders may wonder if they're headed upside down, but they're not. Even though the ride does not have any loops or inversions, its speed gives riders a thrill they will never forget. It reaches speeds of over 90 mph.

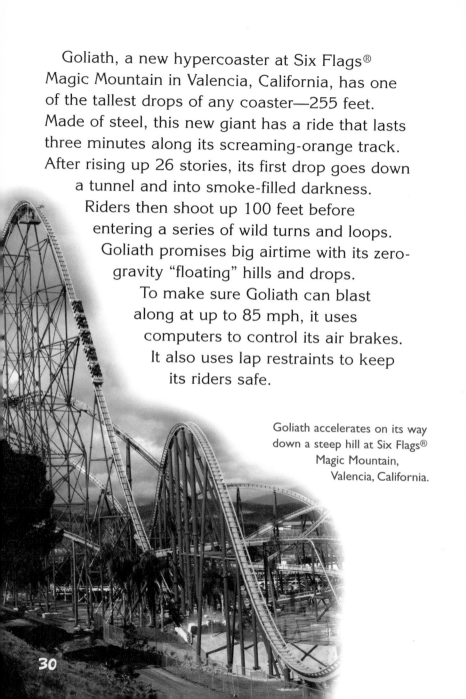

Goliath, a new hypercoaster at Six Flags®
Magic Mountain in Valencia, California, has one
of the tallest drops of any coaster—255 feet.
Made of steel, this new giant has a ride that lasts
three minutes along its screaming-orange track.
After rising up 26 stories, its first drop goes down
a tunnel and into smoke-filled darkness.
Riders then shoot up 100 feet before
entering a series of wild turns and loops.
Goliath promises big airtime with its zero-
gravity "floating" hills and drops.
To make sure Goliath can blast
along at up to 85 mph, it uses
computers to control its air brakes.
It also uses lap restraints to keep
its riders safe.

Goliath accelerates on its way
down a steep hill at Six Flags®
Magic Mountain,
Valencia, California.

The only way to find out which scream machines you think are the best is to try them out. Your idea of a fun ride may not be the same as someone else's. When you try different coasters, you'll see if you like the feel of a woodie as it creaks up the lift hill, seems to want to fly off the track at the top of a hill, and makes lots of noise. You might find that the smooth ride of a bright steelie, with its loops, twists, and big Gs, does the trick for you. You might even like both.

Since the Russians began to build their sliding sleds over 500 years ago, roller coaster designers have been exploring new ways to scare and surprise people. You can choose to scale great heights, blast along at super-fast speeds, and feel your insides seem to flip as you are twisted, turned, and dropped.

For a few minutes on a roller coaster, you can forget about everything except what a wild, wonderful time you're having. If the designer has done a good job, at the end of the ride you'll say, "Let's get back in line for another trip!"

GLOSSARY

acceleration an increase in speed

airtime the feeling of floating at low or negative G-force moments

centripetal force the force that keeps an object moving toward the inside of a circle

compressed air air that is under a pressure greater than the atmosphere's pressure

energy the ability to cause an action

force strength or power exerted upon an object

friction surface resistance to motion

G-forces gravitational force on riders caused by the motion of the coaster as it speeds along

gravity a force of attraction between bodies of matter, as between the mass of the earth and another body that is near its surface

hypercoaster a roller coaster that is higher than 200 feet

inversion a part of the roller coaster that turns riders upside down

lift hill a hill up which coaster cars or trains are hauled

linear induction motor (LIM) a way of launching coaster cars by using magnets

momentum the force of motion

suspended roller coaster a coaster that has enclosed cars that hang beneath the track